mexican
recipes

TRADITIONAL RECIPES FOR THE
PERFECT MEXICAN FEAST

MARLENA SPIELER

This is a Parragon Publishing Book
First published in 2004

Parragon Publishing
Queen Street House
4 Queen Street
Bath BA1 1HE, UK

Created and produced by The Bridgewater Book Company Ltd.

ISBN: 1-40543-162-8

Printed in China

NOTE

*This book uses imperial, metric, and US cup measurements. Follow the same units of
measurement throughout; do not mix metric and imperial. All spoon measurements
are level: teaspoons are assumed to be 5 ml and tablespoons are assumed to be 15 ml.
Unless otherwise stated, milk is assumed to be whole, eggs and individual vegetables
such as potatoes are medium, and pepper is freshly ground black pepper.*

*Ovens should be preheated to the specified temperature. If using a fan-assisted oven,
check the manufacturer's instructions for adjusting the time and temperature.*

*Recipes using raw or very lightly cooked eggs should be avoided by infants, the elderly,
pregnant women, convalescents, and anyone suffering from an illness. Pregnant and
breastfeeding women are advised to avoid eating peanuts and peanut products.*

Contents

Introduction

The cuisine of Mexico is a diverse and extraordinary one, reflecting a complex layering of cultures through history, starting with the indigenous Indian civilizations and built upon by the Spanish conquest, then embracing various other European influences.

The soul of Mexican food lies in its ancient roots, namely Aztec, Toltec, Zapotec, Ohnec, and

through cooking meat makes soups that fuel everyday life and adds flavor and depth to dishes of beans and rice, as well as stews. The wealth of seafood, fished off the thousands of miles of coastlines which define the shape of the country, is eaten cloaked in spicy pastes, or scattered with chiles and wrapped in tortillas or leaves.

Mayan. Deeply colored, complex, rich sauces made of chiles—both mild and hot—and a variety of seeds, herbs, and vegetables are as ancient as the cultures from which they come. Long-stewed meats, such as the Spanish contribution of pork, figure prominently in the Mexican kitchen. The broth that is produced

Over this ancient cuisine of indigenous foods and techniques lies a veneer of Spanish propriety and European tradition, together with the imports from Spain. These include wheat (for those ever-present flour tortillas and the crusty bread rolls, known as *bolillos*); domesticated animals whose milk added cheese to the menu; and not forgetting the noble pig! With the abundant fat provided by the pig, frying became possible, adding new dimensions to the traditional cooking methods.

Mexican Style

Meals in Mexico are a never-ending fiesta—
stimulating to both the eye and the taste buds.

The main meal, the *comida corrida*, is
served, Spanish style, in the afternoon. Breakfast
may either be a light one of soothing hot
chocolate or invigorating coffee, served with
sweet rolls or churros (see page 88 for a recipe)

to dip in, or a hearty late breakfast *almuerzo*,
often consisting of the exquisite egg dishes,
for which Mexico is well known.

The thronging markets and their many
fondas, cantinas, and taquerias then entice
you with their irresistible aromas, convincing
you that you are indeed hungry, even after that
sumptuous breakfast. They never fail to provide
an endless parade of tacos, tostadas, enchiladas,
burritos, soups, shellfish, and grilled fish with
which to tantalize the palate.

And if your appetite becomes jaded by the
sultry heat or, more likely, from all that feasting
on savory delights, and you don't have room for
one more beckoning burrito, persuade yourself
to nibble a reviving snack of a refreshingly
contrasting kind. A slice of fresh fruit is the
perfect answer—luscious pineapple, mango, or
melon. But even simple fruit is given the special
Mexican treatment, sprinkled with hot red pepper
and served with a squeeze of lime juice. After
that, you'll be ready for anything!

The heat of Mexico has produced another
sensory delight: tequila, distilled from a succulent
which grows in abundance in these parts. Try a
margarita to transport you to the sun, or tequila
with ice-cold fruit for a truly decadent quencher.

and warm, a corn tortilla is a soft taco; fried to a crisp, it is a crisp taco. A flat, crisply fried tortilla is known as a tostada, which can then be topped with a layer of refried beans (see below), cheese, pickled chiles, salsa, salad, and tasty morsels of meat or vegetables.

Stale corn tortillas are never thrown away in the frugal Mexican kitchen, and the cuisine is all the better for it. Dipped into spicy sauces, then rolled around various fillings, they make the wonderful casserole that is called enchiladas; or fried and layered with sauce, they are called chilaquiles.

Most of us are now familiar with tortilla chips, at least the kind widely available in packages. But they are at their best when freshly made from stale corn tortillas.

Tortillas

The tortilla—a thin crêpelike flat bread—is eaten at nearly every meal throughout Mexico. Served in the same way as bread to accompany dishes, tortillas are also wrapped around food as an eating utensil.

In the north of Mexico, wheat or flour tortillas will be the ones you find most often, whereas in the south they will be corn, sometimes blue corn. Tortillas vary greatly in size, from tiny to huge, and are either eaten fresh off the grill pan (*comal*) or filled and fried. They form the basis of the foods of Mexico.

Wrapped around any filling, a corn tortilla becomes a taco; a flour tortilla, a burrito. Fresh

Beans

Beans are staples, along with rice and chiles. In every marketplace café (*fonda*) and home kitchen, you'll find pots of simmering beans, ready to be eaten in all their guises, or just from a bowl with a few tortillas to wrap around them to satisfy the hunger.

Throughout Mexico, the types of bean used in cooking vary delightfully, from the tender pale pink beans of the north, such as pinto, to the inky black beans of the south. Beans that are puréed and cooked in fat and spices are called refried beans (see page 34 for a recipe). These are not really fried at all, but cooked down to an intense paste in a puddle of shortening or dripping, or, as is used more commonly in these health-conscious days, vegetable oil.

Chiles

Next to tortillas and beans, it is chiles that most define Mexican food. They offer flavors, textures, colors, and aromas, as well as heat, and keep the often monotonous diet lively. They are consumed raw and cooked, sliced and stewed, stuffed and puréed, soaked and fried, and are eaten at every meal, usually in the form of a salsa to add as desired. They are rich in antioxidant vitamins and will clear your sinuses—and that's not to mention their alleged aphrodisiac qualities.

Understandably, chiles can intimidate—they can be searingly hot, and should be added a little at a time. Mild chiles are generally eaten red and dried, though Mexicans also dote on crushed, hot red chiles—usually in the form of a dried cayenne. Mild chiles, such as pasilla, ancho, mulato, and negro, make up the distinctive flavorful mixture sold simply on our spice shelf as "mild chili powder."

Most fresh chiles are hot and hotter. Jalapeño is probably the most commonly eaten—a good all-purpose little chile with a nice fiery heat and delicious flavor. Serrano is another popular fresh chile. In the Caribbean region, habanero and Scotch bonnet chili peppers add their distinctive fire.

Two milder chiles, the Anaheim and poblano, are delicious eaten stuffed, as you would a bell pepper; if unavailable, use ordinary green bell peppers, roasted and marinated with a chopped fresh hot chile or two to enliven them.

Bottled hot seasonings are ubiquitous, too; you'll find one on practically every table and kitchen shelf—a nice jolt of tangy fire for those who dare.

Other Flavorings

Do not be under the false impression that Mexican spicing is limited to chiles: cinnamon, cloves, black pepper, unsweetened cocoa, and especially cumin are used with enthusiasm, as are the herbs of oregano, marjoram, mint, epazote (a wild herb sold in Latin American markets), and cilantro. Roasted onion and whole garlic cloves are often crushed to form the basis of a sauce, and wedges of lime or lemon are served with soups, meats, fish—in fact, almost everything—in the classic Mediterranean style.

Soups & Appetizers

Spicy Gazpacho

This classic Spanish cold soup is given a Mexican twist by adding chiles and cilantro. Serve with chunks of bread for a refreshing start to a meal.

serves 4–6

1 cucumber

2 green bell peppers

6 ripe flavorful tomatoes

½ fresh hot chile

½–1 onion, finely chopped

3–4 garlic cloves, chopped

4 tbsp extra virgin olive oil

¼ –½ tsp ground cumin

2–4 tsp sherry vinegar

4 tbsp chopped cilantro

2 tbsp chopped fresh parsley

1¼ cups vegetable or chicken stock

2½ cups tomato juice or passata

salt and pepper

ice cubes

crusty bread, to serve

Method

❶ Cut the cucumber in half lengthwise, then cut into fourths. Remove the seeds with a teaspoon, then dice the flesh. Cut the bell peppers in half and remove the cores and seeds, then dice the flesh. (If you prefer to peel the tomatoes, place in a heatproof bowl, then pour boiling water over to cover and let stand for 30 seconds. Drain and plunge into cold water. The skins will then slide off easily.) Cut the tomatoes in half, seed if wished, then chop the flesh. Seed and chop the chile.

❷ In a bowl, combine half the cucumber, green bell pepper, tomatoes, and onion, then place in a food processor or blender with the chile, garlic, oil, cumin, vinegar, and herbs. Process with enough of the stock to form a smooth purée.

❸ Pour the puréed soup into a bowl and stir in the remaining stock and tomato juice. Add the remaining cucumber, green bell pepper, tomatoes, and onion, stirring well. Season to taste with salt and pepper, then cover and chill for a few hours.

❹ Put some ice cubes into each bowl before ladling in the gazpacho. Serve with bread.

Variation

Make the ice cubes by freezing tomato juice as a delicious alternative.

Beef & Vegetable Soup

A wonderful meal-in-a-bowl, this soup is ideal for a winter supper or lunch.
The beefy flavor, enhanced with spices, is very warming.

serves 4–6

8 oz/225 g tomatoes

2 corn on the cob

1 carrot, thinly sliced

1 onion, chopped

1–2 small waxy potatoes, diced

¼ cabbage, thinly sliced

4 cups beef stock or soup

¼ tsp ground cumin

¼ tsp mild chili powder

¼ tsp paprika

8 oz/225 g cooked beef,
cut into bite-size pieces

3–4 tbsp chopped cilantro (optional)

hot salsa, such as Jalapeño Salsa
(see page 24), to serve

Method

❶ To peel the tomatoes, place in a heatproof bowl, then pour boiling water over to cover and let stand for 30 seconds. Drain and plunge into cold water. The skins will then slide off easily. Chop the tomatoes.

❷ Using a large knife, cut the corn on the cob into 1-inch/2.5-cm pieces. Place the tomatoes, carrot, onion, potatoes, cabbage, and stock in a large, heavy-bottom pan. Bring to a boil, then reduce the heat and simmer for 10–15 minutes, or until the vegetables are tender.

❸ Add the corn on the cob pieces, the cumin, chili powder, paprika, and the beef pieces, then return to a boil over medium heat.

❹ Ladle into soup bowls and serve sprinkled with cilantro, if wished, with salsa handed round separately.

Cook's tip

To thicken the soup and give it a flavor of the popular Mexican steamed dumpling known as tamale, add a few tablespoons of masa harina (whole ground white or yellow corn), mixed into a thinnish paste with a little water, along with the corn on the cob pieces, spices, and beef. Stir well, then cook until thickened.

Mexican Vegetable Soup with Tortilla Chips

Crisp tortilla chips act as croutons in this hearty vegetable soup, which is found throughout Mexico. Add cheese to melt in, if you wish.

serves 4–6

2 tbsp vegetable or virgin olive oil

1 onion, finely chopped

4 garlic cloves, finely chopped

¼–½ tsp ground cumin

2–3 tsp mild chili powder, such as ancho or New Mexico

1 carrot, sliced

1 waxy potato, diced

12 oz/350 g fresh or canned tomatoes, diced

1 zucchini, diced

¼ small cabbage, shredded

4 cups vegetable or chicken stock

kernels cut from 1 corn on the cob, or about 4 tbsp canned corn kernels

about 10 green or string beans, cut into bite-size lengths

salt and pepper

To serve

4–6 tbsp chopped cilantro

salsa of your choice or chopped fresh chile, to taste

tortilla chips

Method

❶ Heat the oil in a heavy-bottom pan or sauté pan. Add the onion and garlic and cook for a few minutes until softened, then sprinkle in the cumin and chili powder. Stir in the carrot, potato, tomatoes, zucchini, and cabbage and cook for 2 minutes, stirring occasionally.

❷ Pour in the stock. Cover and cook over medium heat for 10–15 minutes, or until the vegetables are tender. Add extra stock if necessary, then stir in the corn and beans and cook for an additional 5–10 minutes, or until the beans are tender. Season the soup to taste with salt and pepper, bearing in mind that the tortilla chips may be salty.

❸ Ladle the soup into soup bowls and sprinkle each portion with chopped cilantro. Top with a little salsa, then add a handful of tortilla chips.

Cheese & Bean Quesadillas

These bite-size rolls are made from flour tortillas filled with a scrumptious mixture of refried beans, melted cheese, cilantro, and salsa.

serves 4–6

8 flour tortillas

vegetable oil, for oiling

½ quantity Refried Beans (see page 34), warmed with a little water

scant 2 cups grated Cheddar cheese

1 onion, chopped

½ bunch cilantro, chopped, plus a few sprigs to garnish (optional)

1 quantity Salsa Cruda (see page 24)

Method

❶ Make the tortillas pliable by warming them gently in a lightly oiled, nonstick skillet.

❷ Remove the tortillas from the skillet and quickly spread with a layer of warmed beans. Top each tortilla with grated cheese, onion, cilantro, and a spoonful of salsa. Roll up tightly.

❸ Just before serving, heat the nonstick skillet over medium heat, sprinkling lightly with a drop or two of water. Add the tortilla rolls, then cover the skillet and heat through until the cheese melts. Allow to brown lightly, if wished.

❹ Remove from the skillet and slice each roll, on the diagonal, into about 4 bite-size pieces. Serve the dish at once.

Variations

For a more lightweight filling, top each tortilla with florets of lightly cooked broccoli or sautéed, sliced wild mushrooms instead of the beans. Cooked, drained black beans can also be substituted for the Refried Beans. Use Fresh Pineapple Salsa (see page 30) instead of the Salsa Cruda for a change of flavor.

Black Bean Nachos

Packed with authentic Mexican flavors, this tasty black bean and cheese dip is fun to eat and will get any meal off to a good start! As an added bonus, it takes mere minutes to put together if you are using canned beans.

serves 4

8 oz/225 g dried black beans, soaked overnight, or canned black beans, drained

generous 1½–2 cups grated cheese, such as Cheddar, fontina, romano, or Asiago, or a combination

about ¼ tsp cumin seeds or ground cumin

about 4 tbsp sour cream

thinly sliced pickled jalapeño chiles (optional)

1 tbsp chopped cilantro

handful of shredded lettuce

tortilla chips, to serve

Method

❶ If using dried black beans, place the soaked beans in a pan, then cover with fresh water and bring to a boil. Boil for 10 minutes, then reduce the heat to very low and cook gently, covered, for 1½ hours, or until tender. Drain well.

❷ Preheat the oven to 375°F/190°C. Spread the beans in a shallow, ovenproof dish, then scatter the cheese over the top. Sprinkle with cumin to taste.

❸ Bake in the oven for 10–15 minutes, or until the beans are cooked through and the cheese is bubbly and melted.

❹ Remove from the oven and spoon the sour cream on top. Add the jalapeño chiles, if using, and sprinkle with cilantro and lettuce.

❺ Arrange the tortilla chips around the beans, placing them partially in the mixture. Serve the nachos at once.

Variation

To add a meaty flavor, spoon chopped and browned chorizo on top of the beans before sprinkling over the cheese and baking—the combination is excellent. Finely chopped leftover cooked meat can also be added in this way.

Sincronizadas

Once you've tried this Mexican version of a toasted ham and cheese sandwich, you'll never look back! Serve with a tangy salsa and Mexican beer to complete the snack.

serves 6

vegetable oil, for oiling

about 10 flour tortillas

about 1 lb 2 oz/500 g grated cheese

8 oz/225 g cooked ham, diced

salsa of your choice

sour cream sprinkled with chopped fresh herbs, to serve

Method

❶ Lightly oil a nonstick skillet. Off the heat, place a tortilla in the skillet and top with a layer of cheese and ham. Generously spread salsa over another tortilla and place, salsa-side down, on top of the cheese and ham tortilla in the skillet.

❷ Place over medium heat and cook until the cheese is melted and the base of the tortilla is golden brown.

❸ Place a heatproof plate, upside-down, on top of the skillet. Using oven gloves to protect your hands, hold the plate firmly in place and carefully invert the skillet to turn the "sandwich" out onto the plate.

❹ Slide the "sandwich" back into the skillet and cook until the underside of the tortilla is golden brown.

❺ Remove from the skillet and serve, cut into wedges, with sour cream sprinkled with herbs. Repeat with the remaining ingredients.

Variations

For a vegetarian version, cook 4 cups thinly sliced mushrooms in a little olive oil with a crushed garlic clove and use instead of the ham. Alternatively, lightly sauté finely chopped garlic in a little oil, then add rinsed spinach leaves and cook until wilted; chop and substitute for the ham.

Chorizo & Artichoke Heart Quesadillas

Ideal to serve with drinks, these bites are incredibly easy to make—simply top flat tortillas with the ingredients of your choice and pop them under the broiler, then serve in wedges.

serves 4–6

1 chorizo sausage

1 large mild fresh green chile or green bell pepper (optional)

8–10 marinated artichoke hearts or canned artichoke hearts, drained and diced

4 soft corn tortillas, warmed

2 garlic cloves, finely chopped

3 cups grated Cheddar cheese

1 tomato, diced

2 scallions, thinly sliced

1 tbsp chopped cilantro

Method

❶ Preheat the broiler to medium. Dice the chorizo. Heat a heavy-bottom skillet, then add the chorizo and cook until it browns in places.

❷ If using the chile, place under the hot broiler and cook for 10 minutes, or until the skin is charred and the flesh softened. Place in a plastic bag, then twist to seal well and let stand for 20 minutes. Carefully remove the skins from the chile with a knife, then seed and chop the flesh.

❸ Arrange the browned chorizo and the artichoke hearts on the corn tortillas, then transfer half to a baking sheet.

❹ Sprinkle with half the garlic, then half the cheese. Place under the hot broiler and cook until the cheese melts and sizzles. Repeat with the remaining tortillas, garlic, and cheese. Sprinkle the warmed tortillas with the tomato, scallions, chile, if using, and the cilantro. Cut into wedges and serve at once.

Two Classic Salsas

A Mexican meal is not complete without an accompanying salsa. These two traditional salsas are ideal for seasoning any dish, from filled tortillas to grilled meat—they add a spicy hotness that is the very essence of Mexican cooking.

serves 4–6

Jalapeño salsa

1 onion, finely chopped

2–3 garlic cloves, finely chopped

4–6 tbsp roughly chopped pickled jalapeño chiles

juice of ½ lemon

about ¼ tsp ground cumin

salt

Salsa cruda

6–8 ripe tomatoes, finely chopped

scant ½ cup tomato juice

3–4 garlic cloves, finely chopped

½–1 bunch cilantro, coarsely chopped

pinch of sugar

3–4 fresh green chiles, such as jalapeño or serrano, seeded and finely chopped

½–1 tsp ground cumin

3–4 scallions, finely chopped

salt

Method

❶ To make the Jalapeño Salsa, place the onion in a nonmetallic bowl with the garlic, chiles, lemon juice, and cumin. Season to taste with salt and stir together. Cover and chill until required.

❷ To make a chunky-textured Salsa Cruda, stir all the ingredients together in a nonmetallic bowl, adding salt to taste. Cover and chill until required.

❸ To make a smoother-textured Salsa Cruda, process the ingredients in a food processor or blender. Cover and chill until required.

Variation

For the Salsa Cruda, substitute finely chopped orange segments and seeded diced cucumber for the tomatoes, to add a fresh, fruity taste.

Authentic Guacamole

Guacamole is at its best when freshly made, with enough texture to really taste the avocado. Serve as a sauce for anything Mexican, or dip into it with vegetable sticks or tortilla chips.

serves 4

1 ripe tomato

2 limes

2–3 ripe small–medium avocados, or 1–2 large ones

1/4–1/2 onion, finely chopped

pinch of ground cumin

pinch of mild chili powder

1/2–1 fresh green chiles, such as jalapeño or serrano, seeded and finely chopped

1 tbsp finely chopped cilantro, plus extra to garnish (optional)

salt (optional)

tortilla chips, to serve (optional)

Method

❶ To peel the tomato, place in a heatproof bowl, then pour boiling water over to cover and let stand for 30 seconds. Drain and plunge into cold water. The skin will then slide off easily. Cut in half and deseed, then chop the flesh.

❷ Squeeze the juice from the limes into a small, nonmetallic bowl. Cut 1 avocado in half around the pit. Twist apart, then remove the pit with a knife. Carefully peel off the skin, then dice the flesh and toss in the bowl of lime juice to prevent discoloration. Repeat with the remaining avocados. Coarsely mash the avocados.

❸ Add the tomato, onion, cumin, chili powder, chiles, and cilantro to the avocados. If using as a dip for tortilla chips, do not add salt. If using as a sauce, add salt to taste.

❹ To serve the guacamole as a dip, transfer to a serving dish and garnish with cilantro. Serve with tortilla chips.

Mole Poblano

This great Mexican celebration dish, ladled out at village fiestas, baptisms, and weddings, is known for its unusual combination of chiles and chocolate.

serves 8–10

3 dried mulato chiles

3 mild dried ancho chiles

5–6 dried New Mexico or California chiles

1 onion, chopped

5 garlic cloves, chopped

1 lb/450 g ripe tomatoes

2 tortillas, preferably stale, cut into pieces

pinch of cloves

pinch of fennel seeds

$\frac{1}{8}$ tsp each ground cinnamon, coriander, and cumin

3 tbsp lightly toasted sesame seeds

3 tbsp slivered or coarsely ground blanched almonds

2 tbsp raisins

1 tbsp peanut butter (optional)

1¾ cups chicken stock

3–4 tbsp grated bittersweet chocolate, plus extra to garnish

2 tbsp mild chili powder

3 tbsp vegetable oil

salt and pepper

about 1 tbsp lime juice

Method

❶ Using metal tongs, roast each chile over an open flame for a few seconds until the color darkens on all sides, or roast in an unoiled skillet over medium heat for 30 seconds, turning constantly.

❷ Place the roasted chiles in a pan or heatproof bowl and pour over enough boiling water to cover. Cover and let soften for at least 1 hour or overnight. Once or twice, lift the lid and rearrange the chiles so that they soak evenly.

❸ Remove the chiles. Discard the stems and seeds, then cut the flesh into pieces. Place in a food processor or blender.

❹ Add the onion, garlic, tomatoes, tortillas, cloves, fennel seeds, cinnamon, coriander, cumin, sesame seeds, almonds, raisins, and peanut butter, if using. Process to combine. With the motor running, add enough stock through the feeder tube to make a smooth paste. Stir in the remaining stock, chocolate, and chili powder.

❺ Heat the oil in a heavy-bottom pan until smoking, then add the mole mixture—it will splatter as it hits the hot oil. Cook for 10 minutes, stirring occasionally.

❻ Season to taste with salt, pepper, and lime juice. Garnish with chocolate. Serve.

Fresh Pineapple Salsa

This sweet, fruity salsa is fresh and fragrant—a wonderful foil to spicy food from the grill.

serves 4

½ ripe pineapple

juice of 1 lime or lemon

1 garlic clove, finely chopped

1 scallion, thinly sliced

½–1 fresh green or red chile, seeded and finely chopped

½ red bell pepper, seeded and chopped

3 tbsp chopped fresh mint

3 tbsp chopped cilantro

pinch of salt

pinch of sugar

Method

❶ Using a sharp knife, cut off the top and bottom of the pineapple. Place upright on a board, then slice off the skin, cutting downward. Using only half the pineapple, cut the flesh into slices. Halve the slices and remove the cores, if wished. Dice the flesh. Reserve any juice that accumulates as you cut the pineapple.

❷ Place the pineapple and juice in a nonmetallic bowl and stir in the lime juice, garlic, scallion, chile, and red bell pepper.

❸ Add the mint and cilantro, then the salt and sugar. Stir well to combine all the ingredients. Cover and chill until ready to serve.

Variation

Replace the pineapple with 3 juicy oranges, peeled and divided into segments.

Hot Tomato Sauce

This tangy sauce is excellent with crispy tortillas and tostadas, or with grilled or fried fish. Try it instead of ketchup for a change!

serves 4

2–3 fresh green chiles, such as jalapeño
or serrano

8 oz/225 g canned chopped tomatoes

1 scallion, thinly sliced

2 garlic cloves, chopped

2–3 tbsp cider vinegar

¼–⅓ cup water

large pinch of dried oregano

large pinch of ground cumin

large pinch of sugar

large pinch of salt

Method

❶ Slice the chiles open. Remove the seeds if wished, then chop the chiles.

❷ Place the chiles in a food processor or blender with the tomatoes, scallion, garlic, vinegar, water, oregano, cumin, sugar, and salt. Process until smooth.

❸ Adjust the seasoning, then cover and chill the sauce until ready to serve. It will keep for up to 1 week, covered, in the refrigerator.

Cook's tip

If you have sensitive skin, it is advisable to wear rubber gloves when preparing fresh chiles, because the oil in the seeds and flesh can cause irritation. Make sure that you do not touch your eyes when handling cut chiles.

Refried Beans

One of Mexico's most famous dishes, refried beans, or frijoles refritos, is incredibly versatile. Serve them piled onto crisp tostadas or crusty rolls, spooned beside rice or rolled into a tortilla.

serves 4–6

1 lb 2 oz/500 g dried pinto or cranberry beans, soaked overnight and drained

1 fresh mint sprig

1 fresh thyme sprig

1 fresh flatleaf parsley sprig

2–3 onions, chopped

½ cup vegetable oil or generous ½ cup shortening or dripping

½ tsp ground cumin

salt

2¼ cups grated Cheddar cheese (optional)

Method

❶ Place the beans in a pan, then cover with fresh water and add the herb sprigs. Bring to a boil, then reduce the heat to very low and cook gently, covered, for 2 hours, or until tender. Add 1 onion and continue to cook until the onion and beans are very tender.

❷ Place two-thirds of the cooked beans, with their cooking liquid, in a food processor or blender and process to a purée. Stir in the remaining whole beans. Set aside.

❸ Heat the oil in a heavy-bottom skillet. Add the remaining onions and cook until they are very soft. Sprinkle with the cumin and salt to taste.

❹ Ladle in a cupful of the bean mixture, and cook, stirring constantly, until the beans reduce to a thick mixture; the beans will darken slightly as they cook.

❺ Continue adding the bean mixture, a ladleful at a time, stirring and letting the liquid reduce before adding the next ladleful. You should end up with a thick, chunky purée.

❻ If using cheese, sprinkle it over the beans and cover tightly until the heat in the skillet melts the cheese. Alternatively, place under a preheated medium broiler to melt the cheese. Serve at once.

Variation

Add several browned, broken-up chorizo sausages to the beans, along with a small can of sardines, mashed to a paste.

Main

Courses

Chicken Breasts in Green Salsa with Sour Cream

Chicken breasts bathed in a fragrant sauce make a delicate dish, perfect for dinner parties. Serve with rice to complete the meal.

serves 4

4 chicken breast fillets

salt and pepper

all-purpose flour, for dredging

2–3 tbsp butter or a combination of butter and oil

1 lb/450 g mild green salsa or puréed tomatillos

1 cup chicken stock

1–2 garlic cloves, finely chopped

3–5 tbsp chopped cilantro, plus extra to serve

½ fresh green chile, seeded and chopped

½ tsp ground cumin

To serve

1 cup sour cream

several romaine lettuce leaves, shredded

3–5 scallions, thinly sliced

Method

❶ Sprinkle the chicken with salt and pepper to taste, then dredge with flour. Shake off the excess.

❷ Melt the butter in a skillet, then add the chicken and cook over medium–high heat, turning once, until golden but not cooked through—the chicken will continue to cook in the sauce. Remove the chicken from the skillet and set aside.

❸ Place the salsa, stock, garlic, cilantro, chile, and cumin in a pan and bring to a boil. Reduce the heat to a low simmer. Add the chicken to the sauce, spooning the sauce over the chicken. Cook for 25–30 minutes, or until the chicken is cooked through and tender.

❹ Remove the chicken and sauce from the pan and season to taste with salt and pepper. Serve with the sour cream, lettuce, scallions, and cilantro.

Citrus-Marinated Chicken

This is a great dish for a summer meal. The marinade gives the chicken an appetizing flavor and helps keeps it succulent and moist during cooking.

serves 4

1 chicken, cut into 4 pieces

1 tbsp mild chili powder

1 tbsp paprika

2 tsp ground cumin

juice and rind of 1 orange

juice of 3 limes

pinch of sugar

8-10 garlic cloves, finely chopped

1 bunch cilantro, coarsely chopped, plus a few sprigs to garnish

2-3 tbsp extra virgin olive oil

¼ cup beer, tequila, or pineapple juice (optional)

salt and pepper

To serve

lime wedges

tomato, green bell pepper, and scallion salad

Method

❶ Place the chicken in a nonmetallic dish. Mix the remaining ingredients together in a bowl and season to taste.

❷ Pour over the chicken and turn to coat well, then cover and let marinate at room temperature for at least 1 hour. If possible, let marinate in the refrigerator for 24 hours.

❸ Preheat the broiler to medium. Remove the chicken from the marinade and pat dry with paper towels.

❹ Place the chicken on a broiler rack and cook under the hot broiler for 20-25 minutes, turning once, until the chicken is tender and the juices run clear when a skewer is inserted into the thickest part of the meat. Alternatively, cook in a ridged grill pan. Brush with the marinade occasionally, but not for the last few minutes of the cooking time.

❺ Garnish with cilantro sprigs and serve with lime wedges and a tomato, green bell pepper, and scallion salad.

Tequila-Marinated Crispy Chicken Wings

The tequila tenderizes these tasty chicken wings and gives them a delicious flavor. Serve accompanied by corn tortillas, refried beans, salsa, and chilled beer.

serves 4

2 lb/900 g chicken wings

11 garlic cloves, finely chopped

juice of 2 limes

juice of 1 orange

2 tbsp tequila

1 tbsp mild chili powder

2 tsp bottled chipotle salsa or

2 dried chipotle chiles, reconstituted

(see Cook's Tip) and puréed

2 tbsp vegetable oil

1 tsp sugar

¼ tsp ground allspice

pinch of ground cinnamon

pinch of ground cumin

pinch of dried oregano

grilled tomato halves,

to serve (optional)

Method

❶ Cut the chicken wings into 2 pieces at the joint.

❷ Place the chicken wings in a nonmetallic dish and add the remaining ingredients. Toss well to coat, then cover and let marinate in the refrigerator for at least 3 hours or overnight.

❸ Preheat the grill. Cook the chicken over hot coals, turning occasionally, for 15–20 minutes, or until crisply browned and the juices run clear when a skewer is inserted into the thickest part of the meat. Serve at once, with grilled or broiled tomato halves, if wished.

Cook's tip

To reconstitute chipotle chiles, place in a pan and cover with water. Protecting your face against the fumes, bring to a boil. Cook for 5 minutes. Remove from the heat and let stand until softened. Remove and discard the stems and seeds.

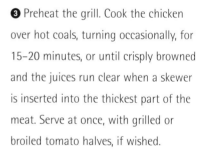

Green Chile & Chicken Chilaquiles

Easy to put together, this dish makes a perfect midweek supper. Use tortilla chips instead of baking the tortillas, if you prefer.

serves 4–6

12 stale tortillas, cut into strips

1 tbsp vegetable oil

1 small cooked chicken, meat removed from the bones and cut into bite-size pieces

Salsa Cruda (see page 24)

3 tbsp chopped cilantro

1 tsp finely chopped fresh oregano or thyme

4 garlic cloves, finely chopped

$\frac{1}{4}$ tsp ground cumin

3 cups grated cheese, such as Cheddar, manchego, or mozzarella

1$\frac{3}{4}$ cups chicken stock

about 1 cup freshly grated Parmesan cheese

To serve

1$\frac{1}{2}$ cups sour cream

3–5 scallions, thinly sliced

pickled chiles

Method

❶ Preheat the oven to 375°F/190°C. Place the tortilla strips in a roasting pan and toss with the oil, then bake for 30 minutes, or until crisp and golden.

❷ Arrange half the chicken in a 9 x 13-inch/23 x 33-cm flameproof casserole, then sprinkle with half the salsa, cilantro, oregano, garlic, cumin, and some of the Cheddar cheese. Repeat these layers and top with the tortilla strips.

❸ Pour the stock over the top, then sprinkle with the Parmesan cheese.

❹ Bake in the oven at the same temperature for 30 minutes, or until heated through and the cheese is lightly golden in places.

❺ Serve with a dollop of sour cream, scallions, and pickled chiles to taste.

Variation

For a vegetarian Mexican filling, add diced sautéed tofu and corn kernels in place of the cooked chicken.

Chicken Tostadas with Green Salsa & Chipotle

Chicken makes a delicate yet satisfying topping for crisp tostadas. You do not need to prepare chicken especially for this recipe—any leftover chicken is equally delicious.

serves 4–6

6 soft corn tortillas

vegetable oil, for frying

1 lb/450 g skinless, boneless chicken breast or thigh, cut into strips or small pieces

1 cup chicken stock

2 garlic cloves, finely chopped

14 oz/400 g Refried Beans (see page 34) or canned pinto or cranberry beans

large pinch of ground cumin

2 cups grated cheese

1 tbsp chopped cilantro

2 ripe tomatoes, diced

handful of crisp lettuce leaves, such as romaine or crisphead, shredded

4–6 radishes, diced

3 scallions, thinly sliced

1 ripe avocado, pitted, peeled, diced, and tossed with lime juice

sour cream, to taste

1–2 canned chipotle chiles in adobo marinade or reconstituted dried chipotle, (see Cook's Tip, page 42), cut into thin strips

Method

❶ To make the tostadas, cook the tortillas in a small amount of oil in a nonstick skillet until crisp. Set aside.

❷ Place the chicken in a pan with the stock and garlic. Bring to a boil, then reduce the heat and cook for 1–2 minutes, or until the chicken begins to turn opaque.

❸ Remove the chicken from the heat and let stand in its hot liquid to cook through.

❹ Heat the beans in a separate pan with enough water to form a smooth purée. Add the cumin and keep warm.

❺ Reheat the tostadas under a preheated medium broiler. Spread the hot beans on the tostadas, then sprinkle with the grated cheese. Lift the cooked chicken from the liquid and divide between the tostadas. Top with the cilantro, tomatoes, lettuce, radishes, scallions, avocado, sour cream, and a few strips of chipotle. Serve at once.

Classic Beef Fajitas

Sizzling strips of marinated meat rolled up in soft flour tortillas with a tangy salsa are perfect for relaxed entertaining. A lettuce and orange salad would go well, too.

serves 4–6

1 lb 9 oz/700 g sirloin steak or other tender steak, cut into strips

3 garlic cloves, chopped

juice of ½ lime

large pinch of mild chili powder

large pinch of paprika

large pinch of ground cumin

1–2 tbsp extra virgin olive oil

salt and pepper

12 flour tortillas

vegetable oil, for oiling and frying

1–2 ripe avocados, pitted, peeled, diced, and tossed with lime juice

½ cup sour cream

Pico de gallo salsa

8 ripe tomatoes, diced

3 scallions, sliced

1–2 fresh green chiles, such as jalapeño or serrano, seeded and chopped

3–4 tbsp chopped cilantro

5–8 radishes, diced

ground cumin, to taste

Method

❶ Combine the steak with the garlic, lime juice, chili powder, paprika, cumin, oil, and salt and pepper to taste. Mix well. Cover and let marinate for 30 minutes at room temperature, or overnight in the refrigerator.

❷ To make the Pico de Gallo Salsa, place the tomatoes in a bowl with the scallions, chiles, cilantro, and radishes. Season to taste with cumin, salt, and pepper. Set aside.

❸ Heat the tortillas in a lightly oiled, nonstick skillet; wrap in foil or a clean dish towel as you work, to keep them warm.

❹ Heat a little oil in a large skillet or preheated wok. Add the beef and stir-fry over high heat until browned and just cooked through.

❺ Serve the sizzling hot meat with the warmed tortillas, salsa, avocado, and sour cream for each person to make his or her own rolled-up fajitas.

Michoacan Beef

This rich, smoky-flavored stew is delicious; leftovers make a great filling for tacos, too.

serves 4–6

about 3 tbsp all-purpose flour

salt and pepper

2 lb 4 oz/1 kg stewing beef, cut into large bite-size pieces

2 tbsp vegetable oil

2 onions, chopped

5 garlic cloves, chopped

14 oz/400 g tomatoes, diced

1½ dried chipotle chiles, reconstituted (see Cook's Tip, page 42) and cut into thin strips

6¼ cups beef stock

12 oz/350 g green beans

pinch of sugar

To serve

red kidney beans

steamed rice

Method

❶ Place the flour in a large bowl and season to taste with salt and pepper. Add the beef and toss to coat well. Remove the beef from the bowl, shaking off the excess flour.

❷ Heat the oil in a skillet. Add the beef and brown briefly over high heat. Reduce the heat to medium, then add the onions and garlic and cook for 2 minutes.

❸ Add the tomatoes, chiles, and stock, then cover and simmer over low heat for 1½ hours, or until the meat is very tender, adding the green beans and sugar 15 minutes before the end of the cooking time. Skim off any fat that rises to the surface every now and again.

❹ Transfer to individual bowls and serve with red kidney beans and rice.

Cook's tip

This is traditionally made with nopales—edible cacti—which gives the dish a distinctive flavor. If you can find these, you need 12–14 oz/ 350–400 g canned nopales, or fresh ones, peeled, sliced, and blanched. Add them with the tomatoes.

Carnitas

In this classic Mexican dish, pieces of pork are first simmered to make them
meltingly tender, then browned until irresistibly crisp.

serves 4–6

2 lb 4 oz/1 kg pork, such as lean belly

1 onion, chopped

1 whole garlic bulb, cut in half

½ tsp ground cumin

2 meat stock cubes

2 bay leaves

salt and pepper

fresh chile strips, to garnish

To serve

freshly cooked rice

Refried Beans (see page 34)

salsa of your choice

Method

❶ Place the pork in a heavy-bottom pan
with the onion, garlic, cumin, stock cubes,
and bay leaves. Add water to cover. Bring
to a boil, then reduce the heat to very low.
Skim off the scum that rises to the
surface.

❷ Continue to cook very gently for
2 hours, or until the pork is tender.
Remove from the heat and let the pork
cool in the liquid.

❸ Remove the pork from the pan with
a slotted spoon. Cut off any rind (roast
separately to make crackling), then cut
the pork into bite-size pieces and sprinkle
with salt and pepper to taste. Reserve
1¼ cups of the cooking liquid.

❹ Brown the pork in a heavy-bottom
skillet for 15 minutes, to cook out the fat.
Add the reserved cooking liquid and let
reduce down. Continue to cook the meat
for 15 minutes, covering the skillet to
avoid splattering. Turn the pork every now
and again.

❺ Transfer the pork to a serving dish, then
garnish with chile strips. Serve with rice,
Refried Beans, and salsa.

Spicy Pork with Prunes

Prunes add an earthy, wine flavor to this spicy stew. Serve with tortillas or crusty bread to dip into the rich sauce.

serves 4–6

1 pork joint, such as leg or shoulder, weighing 3 lb 5 oz/1.5 kg

juice of 2–3 limes

10 garlic cloves, chopped

3–4 tbsp mild chili powder, such as ancho or New Mexico

4 tbsp vegetable oil

salt

2 onions, chopped

generous 2 cups chicken stock

25 small tart tomatoes, coarsely chopped

25 ready-to-eat prunes, pitted

1–2 tsp sugar

pinch of ground cinnamon

pinch of ground allspice

pinch of ground cumin

warmed soft corn tortillas, to serve

Method

❶ Combine the pork with the lime juice, garlic, chili powder, and half the oil in a nonmetallic bowl or dish, and season to taste with salt. Cover and let marinate in the refrigerator overnight.

❷ Preheat the oven to 350°F/180°C. Remove the pork from the marinade. Wipe the pork dry with paper towels and reserve the marinade. Heat the remaining oil in a flameproof casserole and brown the pork evenly until just golden. Add the onions, the reserved marinade, and the stock. Cover and cook in the oven for 2–3 hours, or until tender.

❸ Remove the casserole from the oven and spoon off the fat from the surface of the cooking liquid. Add the tomatoes.

Return to the oven for 20 minutes, or until the tomatoes are tender. Remove the casserole from the oven. Mash the tomatoes into a rough purée. Add the prunes and sugar. Adjust the seasoning, adding cinnamon, allspice, and cumin, as well as extra chili powder, if wished.

❹ Increase the oven temperature to 400°F/200°C and return the casserole to the oven for an additional 20–30 minutes, or until the meat has browned on top and the juices have thickened.

❺ Remove the meat from the casserole and let stand for a few minutes. Carefully carve the joint into thin slices and spoon the sauce over the top. Serve warm, with corn tortillas.

Chile Verde

If tomatillos are not available, use fresh tomatoes and bottled green salsa instead, and add a good hit of lime juice at the end.

serves 4

2 lb 4 oz/1 kg pork, cut into
bite-size pieces
1 onion, chopped
2 bay leaves
1 whole garlic bulb, cut in half
1 meat stock cube
2 garlic cloves, chopped
1 lb/450 g fresh tomatillos, husks removed,
cooked in a small amount of water until
just tender, then chopped; or canned
tomatillos
2 large fresh mild green chiles, such as
Anaheim, seeded and chopped

3 tbsp vegetable oil
1 cup pork or chicken stock
½ tsp mild chili powder, such as
ancho or New Mexico
½ tsp ground cumin
4–6 tbsp chopped cilantro,
to garnish

To serve
warmed flour tortillas
lime wedges

Method

❶ Place the pork in a large, flameproof casserole with the onion, bay leaves, and garlic bulb. Add water to cover and the stock cube and bring to a boil. Skim off the scum that rises to the surface, then reduce the heat to very low and simmer gently for 1½ hours, or until the meat is very tender.

❷ Meanwhile, place the chopped garlic in a food processor or blender with the tomatillos and chiles, then process to a purée.

❸ Heat the oil in a deep sauté pan. Add the tomatillo mixture and cook over medium–high heat for 10 minutes, or until thickened. Add the stock, chili powder, and cumin.

❹ Remove the meat from the casserole and add to the sauce. Simmer gently for 20 minutes.

❺ Garnish with the chopped cilantro and serve with warmed tortillas and lime wedges.

Burritos of Lamb & Black Beans

Stir-fried marinated lamb strips are paired with earthy black beans in these tasty burritos.

serves 4

1 lb 7 oz/650 g lean lamb, thinly sliced

3 garlic cloves, finely chopped

juice of ½ lime

½ tsp mild chili powder

½ tsp ground cumin

large pinch of dried oregano

1–2 tbsp extra virgin olive oil

salt and pepper

14 oz/400 g cooked black beans, seasoned with a little cumin, salt, and pepper

4 large flour tortillas

2–3 tbsp chopped cilantro, plus a few sprigs to garnish

bottled chipotle salsa or salsa of your choice

lime wedges, to serve (optional)

Method

❶ Combine the lamb with the garlic, lime juice, chili powder, cumin, oregano, and oil in a nonmetallic bowl. Season to taste with salt and pepper. Cover and let marinate in the refrigerator for 4 hours.

❷ Warm the beans with a little water in a pan.

❸ Heat the tortillas in an unoiled, nonstick skillet, sprinkling them with a few drops of water as they heat; wrap the tortillas in foil or a clean dish towel as you work, to keep them warm. (Alternatively, stack them in the skillet, moving them from the top to the bottom so that they warm evenly. Wrap to keep warm.)

❹ Stir-fry the lamb in a heavy-bottom, nonstick skillet over high heat until browned on all sides. Remove the skillet from the heat.

❺ Spoon some of the beans and browned meat into a tortilla and sprinkle with cilantro, then add a little salsa and fold in the sides. Repeat with the remaining tortillas. Garnish with cilantro sprigs and serve at once with lime wedges and any spare salsa, if wished.

Variation

Add a spoonful or two of cooked rice to each burrito.

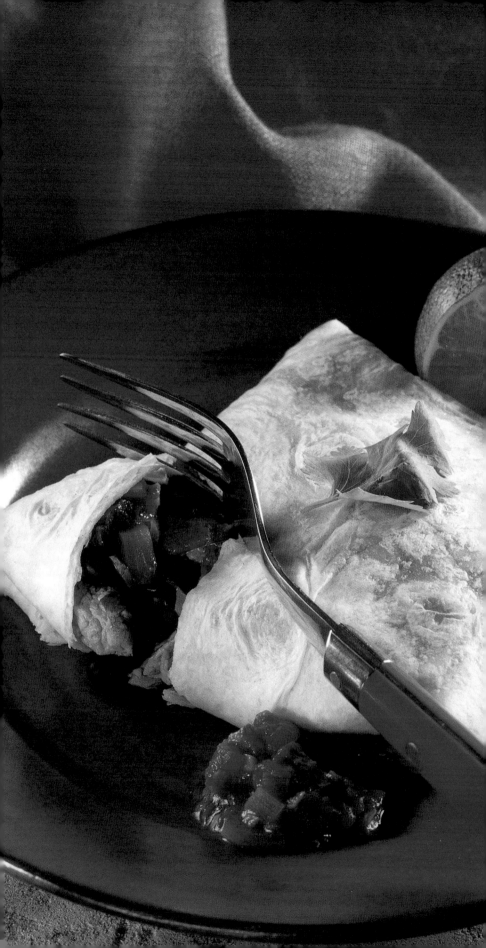

Spicy Meat & Chipotle Hash

This specialty from the town of Puebla in Mexico makes divine soft tacos: simply serve with a stack of warmed soft corn tortillas and let everyone roll their own, fajita-style.

serves 6

1 tbsp vegetable oil

1 onion, finely chopped

1 lb/450 g leftover meat, such as simmered pork or beef, cooled and cut into thin strips

1 tbsp mild chili powder

2 ripe tomatoes, seeded and diced

about 1 cup meat stock

½–1 canned chipotle chile, mashed, plus a little of the marinade, or a few shakes of bottled chipotle salsa

chopped cilantro, to garnish, plus extra to serve

To serve

warmed soft corn tortillas

½ cup sour cream

4–6 tbsp chopped radishes

3–4 crisp lettuce leaves, such as romaine or crisphead, shredded

Method

❶ Heat the oil in a skillet. Add the onion and cook until softened, stirring occasionally. Add the meat and cook for 3 minutes, or until lightly browned, stirring.

❷ Add the chili powder, tomatoes, and stock and cook until the tomatoes reduce to a sauce; mash the meat a little as it cooks.

❸ Add the chipotle and marinade and continue to cook and mash until the sauce and meat are nearly blended.

❹ Garnish with cilantro and serve with a stack of warmed corn tortillas so that people can fill them with the meat mixture to make tacos. Also serve sour cream, extra cilantro, radishes, and lettuce for each person to add to the meat.

Cook's tip

Avocados add an interesting texture contrast to the spicy meat—serve with 2 sliced avocados, tossed with lime juice. Try serving on top of tostadas instead of wrapping taco-style.

Spicy Broiled Salmon

The woody smoked flavors of the chipotle chile are delicious brushed onto salmon for broiling. The marinade goes just as well with fresh tuna steaks.

serves 4

4 salmon steaks, about 6–8 oz/
175–225 g each

To serve

tomato wedges

3 scallions, finely chopped

shredded lettuce

Marinade

4 garlic cloves, finely chopped

2 tbsp extra virgin olive oil

pinch of ground allspice

pinch of ground cinnamon

juice of 2 limes

1–2 tsp marinade from canned chipotle chiles or bottled chipotle salsa

¼ tsp ground cumin

pinch of sugar

salt and pepper

lime slices, to garnish

Method

❶ To make the marinade, place the garlic, oil, allspice, cinnamon, lime juice, chipotle marinade, cumin, and sugar in a nonmetallic bowl. Add salt and pepper to taste and stir well.

❷ Coat the salmon with the garlic mixture, then transfer to a large, nonmetallic dish. Cover with plastic wrap and let marinate in the refrigerator for 1 hour.

❸ Preheat the broiler to medium. Transfer the salmon steaks to a broiler rack and cook under the hot broiler for 3–4 minutes on each side, or until cooked through. Alternatively, grill the salmon steaks.

❹ To serve, mix the tomato wedges with the scallions. Place the salmon on individual plates and arrange the tomato salad and lettuce alongside. Garnish with lime slices and serve at once.

Fish with Yucatan Flavors

Annatto seeds are rock hard little red seeds that need to be soaked overnight before you can grind them. They have a distinctive lemony flavor and impart a dark orange color to the dish.

serves 8

4 tbsp annatto seeds, soaked in
water overnight

3 garlic cloves, finely chopped

1 tbsp mild chili powder

1 tbsp paprika

1 tsp ground cumin

½ tsp dried oregano

2 tbsp beer or tequila

juice of 1 lime and 1 orange

2 tbsp olive oil

2 tbsp chopped cilantro,
plus a few sprigs to garnish

¼ tsp ground cinnamon

¼ tsp ground cloves

2 lb 4 oz/1 kg swordfish steaks

banana leaves, for wrapping (optional)

orange wedges, to serve

Method

❶ Drain the annatto, then crush them to a paste with a pestle and mortar. Work in the garlic, chili powder, paprika, cumin, oregano, beer, fruit juice, oil, cilantro, cinnamon, and cloves.

❷ Smear the paste onto the fish, then cover and let marinate in the refrigerator for at least 3 hours or overnight.

❸ Wrap the fish steaks in the banana leaves, tying with string to make packages. Bring enough water to a boil in a steamer, then add a batch of packages to the top part of the steamer and steam for

15 minutes, or until the fish is cooked through.

❹ Alternatively, cook the fish without wrapping in the banana leaves. To cook on the grill, place in a hinged basket, or on a rack, and cook over hot coals for 5–6 minutes on each side, or until cooked through. Alternatively, cook the fish under a broiler for 5–6 minutes on each side, or until cooked through.

❺ Garnish with cilantro sprigs and serve with orange wedges for squeezing over the fish.

Chile-Marinated Shrimp with Avocado Sauce

Avocado salsa is delicious spooned onto anything spicy from the grill or broiler, especially seafood.

serves 4

1 lb 7 oz/650 g raw jumbo shrimp, shelled and tails left intact

½ tsp ground cumin

½ tsp mild chili powder

½ tsp paprika

2 tbsp orange juice

grated rind of 1 orange

2 tbsp extra virgin olive oil

2 tbsp chopped cilantro, plus extra to garnish

salt and pepper

2 ripe avocados

½ onion, finely chopped

¼ fresh green or red chile, seeded and chopped

juice of ½ lime

Method

❶ Preheat the grill. Mix the shrimp, cumin, chili powder, paprika, orange juice and rind, oil, and half the cilantro. Season to taste with salt and pepper.

❷ Thread the shrimp onto metal skewers, or bamboo skewers that have been soaked in cold water for 30 minutes.

❸ Cut the avocados in half around the pit. Twist apart, then remove the pit with a knife. Carefully peel off the skin, then dice the flesh and toss with the remaining cilantro, and the onion, chile, and lime juice in a nonmetallic bowl. Season to taste with salt and pepper and set aside.

❹ Place the shrimp over the hot coals of the grill and cook for only a few minutes on each side, or until bright pink and opaque.

❺ Garnish the shrimp with cilantro and serve with the avocado sauce.

Variation

For luscious sandwiches, toast crusty rolls, halved and buttered, over the hot coals and fill them with the cooked shrimp and avocado sauce.

Migas

A great brunch or supper dish, made by scrambling eggs with chiles, tomatoes, and tortilla chips. Try it with sour cream to melt over the eggs.

serves 4

2 tbsp butter

6 garlic cloves, finely chopped

1 fresh green chile, such as jalapeño or serrano, seeded and diced

1½ tsp ground cumin

6 ripe tomatoes, coarsely chopped

8 eggs, lightly beaten

8–10 soft corn tortillas, cut into strips and fried until crisp, or an equal amount of not too salty tortilla chips

4 tbsp chopped cilantro

3–4 scallions, thinly sliced

mild chili powder, to garnish

Method

❶ Melt half the butter in a pan. Add the garlic and chile and cook until softened but not browned. Add the cumin and cook for 30 seconds, stirring, then add the chopped tomatoes and cook over medium heat for an additional 3–4 minutes, or until the tomato juices have evaporated. Remove from the pan and set aside. Melt the remaining butter in a skillet over low heat and pour in the beaten eggs. Cook, stirring, until the eggs begin to set.

❷ Add the reserved chile tomato mixture to the skillet, stirring gently to mix into the eggs.

❸ Carefully add the fried tortilla strips and continue cooking, stirring once or twice, until the eggs are the consistency you wish. The tortillas should be pliable and chewy.

❹ Transfer to a serving plate and surround with the cilantro and scallions. Garnish with a sprinkling of chili powder and serve.

Variation

Add browned ground beef or pork to the softly scrambling egg mixture. A bunch of cooked chopped spinach or Swiss chard can be stirred in as well, to add fresh color.

Rice with Black Beans

Any kind of bean cooking liquid is delicious for cooking rice—black beans are particularly good for their startling pinkish-gray color and earthy flavor.

serves 4

1 onion, chopped

5 garlic cloves, chopped

1 cup chicken or vegetable stock

2 tbsp vegetable oil

scant 1 cup long-grain rice

1 cup liquid from cooking black beans,
plus a handful of beans

½ tsp ground cumin

salt and pepper

To garnish

3–5 scallions, thinly sliced

2 tbsp chopped cilantro

Method

❶ Place the onion in a food processor or blender with the garlic and stock and process until the consistency of a chunky sauce.

❷ Heat the oil in a heavy-bottom skillet and cook the rice until it is golden. Add the onion mixture with the bean cooking liquid and the beans. Add the cumin and salt and pepper to taste.

❸ Cover the skillet and cook over medium–low heat for 10 minutes, or until the rice is just tender. The rice should be a pinkish-gray color and taste delicious.

❹ Fluff up the rice with a fork, then cover and let stand for 5 minutes. Serve sprinkled with scallions and cilantro.

Variation

Instead of black beans, use pinto beans or chickpeas. Proceed as above and serve with any savory spicy sauce, or as an accompaniment to roasted meat.

Vegetable Tostadas

Top a crisp tostada with spicy vegetables and you have a fabulous vegetarian feast.

serves 4

4 soft corn tortillas

2-3 tbsp virgin olive oil or vegetable oil, plus extra for frying

2 potatoes, diced

1 carrot, diced

3 garlic cloves, finely chopped

1 red bell pepper, seeded and diced

1 tsp mild chili powder

1 tsp paprika

½ tsp ground cumin

3-4 ripe tomatoes, diced

¾ cup green beans, blanched and cut into bite-size lengths

several large pinches of dried oregano

14 oz/400 g cooked black beans, drained

8 oz/225 g feta cheese (drained weight), crumbled

3-4 romaine lettuce leaves, shredded

3-4 scallions, thinly sliced

Method

❶ To make the tostadas, cook the tortillas in a small amount of oil in a nonstick skillet until crisp. Set aside.

❷ Heat the remaining oil in the skillet. Add the potatoes and carrot and cook for 10 minutes, or until softened. Add the garlic, red bell pepper, chili powder, paprika, and cumin. Cook for 2-3 minutes, or until the bell peppers have softened.

❸ Add the tomatoes, green beans, and oregano. Cook for 8-10 minutes, or until the vegetables are tender and form a saucelike mixture. The mixture should not be too dry; add a little water if necessary to keep it moist.

❹ Preheat the broiler to medium. Heat the black beans in a pan with a tiny amount of water and keep warm. Reheat the tostadas under the hot broiler.

❺ Layer the beans over the hot tostadas, then sprinkle with the cheese and top with a few spoonfuls of the hot vegetables in sauce. Sprinkle each tostada with the lettuce and scallions and serve at once.

Cheese Enchiladas with Mole Flavors

Mole sauce makes a delicious enchilada—a good reason to make yourself a big pot of Mole Poblano (see page 28). But if you are short of time, you can always use bottled mole paste instead.

serves 4–6

8 soft corn tortillas

vegetable oil, for oiling

1¾ cups Mole Poblano
(see page 28) or bottled mole paste

about 2 cups grated cheese, such as
Cheddar, mozzarella, Asiago, or Oaxaca,
or a combination

1 cup chicken or vegetable stock

5 scallions, thinly sliced

2–3 tbsp chopped cilantro

handful of romaine lettuce leaves,
shredded

1 ripe avocado, pitted, peeled, diced, and
tossed in lime juice

4 tbsp sour cream

salsa of your choice

Method

❶ Preheat the oven to 375°F/190°C. Heat the tortillas in a lightly oiled, nonstick skillet; wrap the tortillas in foil or a clean dish towel as you work, to keep them warm.

❷ Dip the tortillas into the mole sauce and pile up on a plate. Fill the inside of the top sauced tortilla with a few spoonfuls of grated cheese. Roll up and arrange in a shallow, ovenproof dish. Repeat with the remaining tortillas, reserving a handful of the cheese to sprinkle over the top.

❸ Pour the rest of the mole sauce over the rolled tortillas, then pour the stock over the top. Sprinkle with the reserved cheese and cover with foil.

❹ Bake in the oven for 20 minutes, or until the tortillas are piping hot and the cheese filling melts.

❺ Remove the foil. Arrange the scallions, cilantro, lettuce, avocado, and sour cream on top. Add salsa to taste and serve at once.

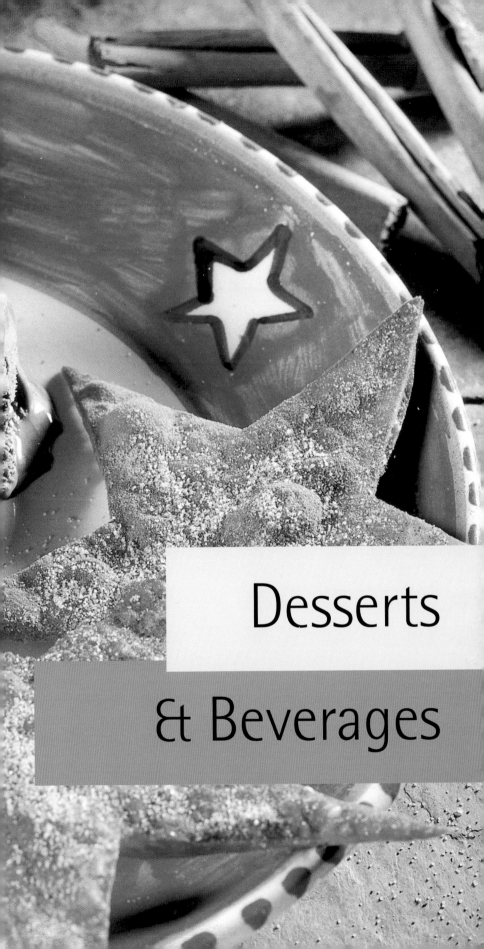

Desserts
& Beverages

Icy Fruit Blizzard

Keep a store of prepared fruit in the freezer, then whirl it up into this refreshing dessert, which is as light and healthy as it is satisfying. Vary the fruit as you like.

serves 4

1 pineapple

1 large piece watermelon, peeled, seeded and cut into small pieces

8 oz/225 g strawberries or other berries, hulled and left whole or sliced

1 mango, peach, or nectarine, pitted, peeled, and sliced

1 banana, peeled and sliced

orange juice

superfine sugar, to taste

Method

❶ Using a sharp knife, cut off the top and bottom of the pineapple. Place upright on a board, then slice off the skin, cutting downward. Cut in half, remove the core if wished, then cut the flesh into small chunks.

❷ Cover 2 baking sheets with plastic wrap. Arrange all the fruit on top. Open freeze for at least 2 hours, or until firm and icy.

❸ Put one type of fruit in a food processor or blender and process until it is broken up into small pieces.

❹ Add a little orange juice and sugar to taste, and continue to process until it forms a granular mixture. Repeat with the remaining fruit. Arrange in chilled bowls and serve at once.

Variation

For an icy fruit yogurt shake, omit the pineapple and watermelon and process the remaining fruit together, replacing the juice with a half-and-half mix of milk and fruit yogurt.

Pineapple with Tequila & Mint

This light, chilled dessert is a refreshing way to finish a Mexican spread.
For a more elaborate dish, accompany the pineapple with a
scoop of good-quality pineapple sherbet.

serves 4–6

1 pineapple

sugar, to taste

juice of 1 lemon

2–3 tbsp tequila or a few drops of
vanilla extract

several sprigs of fresh mint, leaves
removed and cut into thin strips

fresh mint sprig, to decorate

Method

❶ Using a sharp knife, cut off the top and bottom of the pineapple. Place upright on a board, then slice off the skin, cutting downward. Cut in half, remove the core if wished, then cut the flesh into chunks.

❷ Place the pineapple in a bowl and sprinkle with the sugar, lemon juice, and tequila.

❸ Toss the pineapple to coat well, then cover and chill until ready to serve.

❹ To serve, arrange on a serving plate and sprinkle with the mint strips. Decorate the dish with a mint sprig.

Variation

Substitute 3 mangoes for the pineapple.
To prepare the mangoes, slice off a large piece
of flesh on either side of the pit of each fruit.
Peel and cut into chunks. Slice off the
remaining flesh attached to the pit.

Aztec Oranges

**Simplicity itself, this refreshing orange dessert is hard to beat
and is the perfect follow-up to a hearty, spiced main course.**

serves 4–6

6 oranges	soft dark brown sugar, to taste
1 lime	fine lime rind strips, to decorate
2 tbsp tequila	(see Cook's Tip)
2 tbsp orange-flavored liqueur	

Method

❶ Using a sharp knife, cut a slice off the top and bottom of the oranges, then remove the peel and pith, cutting downward and taking care to retain the shape of the oranges.

❷ Holding the oranges on their side, cut them horizontally into slices.

❸ Place the oranges in a nonmetallic bowl. Cut the lime in half and squeeze over the oranges. Sprinkle with the tequila and liqueur, then sprinkle over sugar to taste.

❹ Cover and chill until ready to serve, then transfer to a serving dish and decorate with lime rind strips.

Cook's tip

To make the decoration, finely pare the rind from a lime using a vegetable peeler, then cut into thin strips. Add to boiling water and blanch for 2 minutes. Drain in a strainer and rinse under cold running water. Drain again and pat dry with paper towels. Use this method for decorative orange and lemon rind strips as well.

Strawberries & Oranges with Lime

An ideal summer dessert, or try it with brunch. The oranges enhance the flavor of the berries. A hint of orange-flavored liqueur is divine (reduce or omit the sugar).

serves 4

3 sweet oranges

8 oz/225 g strawberries

grated rind and juice of 1 lime

1–2 tbsp superfine sugar

To decorate

fine lime rind strips

(see Cook's Tip, page 82)

fresh mint sprig

Method

❶ Using a sharp knife, cut a slice off the top and bottom of the oranges, then remove the peel and pith, cutting downward and taking care to retain the shape of the oranges.

❷ Using a small sharp knife, cut down between the membranes of the oranges to remove the segments. Discard the membranes.

❸ Hull the strawberries, pulling the leaves off with a pinching action. Cut into slices along the length of the strawberries.

❹ Place the oranges and strawberries in a nonmetallic bowl, then sprinkle with the lime rind and juice and sugar. Cover and chill until ready to serve.

❺ To serve, transfer to a serving bowl. Decorate the dish with lime rind strips and a mint sprig.

Variation

Replace the oranges with mangoes, and the strawberries with blackberries, for a dramatically colored dessert.

Mexican Chocolate Meringues

The Mexican name for these delicate meringues is suspiros, meaning "sighs"— supposedly the contented sighs of the nuns who created them. They are lightly crisp on the outside, with deliciously chewy centres.

makes about 25 meringues

4–5 egg whites, at room temperature

pinch of salt

¼ tsp cream of tartar

¼–½ tsp vanilla extract

generous ¾ cup–1 cup superfine sugar

⅛–¼ tsp ground cinnamon

4 squares bittersweet chocolate, grated

To serve

ground cinnamon

bittersweet chocolate pieces, half-melted

whipped cream

4 oz/115 g strawberries

Method

❶ Preheat the oven to 300°F/150°C. Whisk the egg whites in a large bowl until they are foamy, then add the salt and cream of tartar and beat until very stiff. Whisk in the vanilla extract, then slowly whisk in the sugar, a small amount at a time, until the meringue is shiny and stiff. This should take about 3 minutes by hand, and under 1 minute with an electric beater.

❷ Whisk in the cinnamon and grated chocolate. Spoon mounds of about 2 tablespoonfuls onto an ungreased, non-stick baking sheet. Space the mounds well. Bake in the oven for 2 hours, or until set.

❸ Carefully remove from the baking sheet. If the meringues are too moist and soft, return them to the oven to firm up and dry out more. Let cool completely.

❹ To serve, dust the meringues with cinnamon. Stir the half-melted chocolate pieces into stiffly whipped cream and serve, with strawberries, alongside the meringues.

Churros

Sold on the streets of Mexico, these tempting treats can be enjoyed at any time of the day—dip them into a cup of hot chocolate for breakfast, nibble them as a midday snack with coffee, or serve them as part of a late-night supper.

serves 4

1 cup water

rind of 1 lemon

6 tbsp butter

⅛ tsp salt

generous ¾ cup all-purpose flour

¼ tsp ground cinnamon, plus extra for dusting

½–1 tsp vanilla extract

3 eggs

vegetable oil, for frying

superfine sugar, for dusting

Method

❶ Place the water with the lemon rind in a heavy-bottom pan. Bring to a boil, then add the butter and salt and cook for a few moments until the butter melts.

❷ Add the flour all at once with the cinnamon and vanilla extract, then remove the pan from the heat and stir rapidly until it forms the consistency of mashed potatoes.

❸ Beat in the eggs, one at a time, using a wooden spoon; if you have difficulty, use a potato masher, and when it is mixed, return to using a wooden spoon and continue to mix until smooth.

❹ Heat 1 inch/2.5 cm of oil in a large, heavy-bottom skillet to 350–375°F/ 180–190°C, or until a cube of bread browns in 30 seconds.

❺ Place the batter in a pastry bag fitted with a wide star nozzle, then squeeze out in 5-inch/13-cm lengths directly into the hot oil, making sure that the churros are about 3–4 inches/7.5–10 cm apart, since they will puff up as they cook. You may need to cook them in 2–3 batches.

❻ Cook the churros in the hot oil for 2 minutes on each side, or until they are golden brown. Remove with a slotted spoon and drain on kitchen paper.

❼ Dust generously with sugar and sprinkle with cinnamon to taste. Serve either hot or at room temperature.

Buñuelo Stars

Cutting the flour tortillas into star shapes makes a whimsical treat, and the points of the stars get deliciously crisp. Serve with ice cream or sundaes.

serves 4

4 flour tortillas

3 tbsp ground cinnamon

6–8 tbsp superfine sugar

vegetable oil, for frying

To serve

chocolate ice cream

fine orange rind strips

(see Cook's Tip, page 82)

Method

❶ Using a sharp knife or kitchen scissors, cut each tortilla into star shapes.

❷ Mix the cinnamon and sugar together in a bowl and set aside.

❸ Heat 1 inch/2.5 cm of oil in a large, heavy-bottom skillet to 350–375°F/ 180–190°C, or until a cube of bread browns in 30 seconds. Working one at a time, cook the shapes until one side is golden. Turn and cook until golden on the other side. Remove from the hot oil with a slotted spoon and drain on paper towels.

❹ Sprinkle the buñuelos generously with the cinnamon and sugar mixture. Serve with chocolate ice cream, sprinkled with orange rind strips.

Variation

Drench the buñuelos in a simple syrup, flavored with a little cinnamon or aniseed.

Classic Margaritas

Margaritas are what make a hot and sultry Mexican afternoon not only tolerable but something to look forward to—a tropical holiday in a glass.

serves 2

Classic margaritas

pared lime or lemon rind

salt, for dipping

3 tbsp tequila

3 tbsp orange-flavored liqueur

3 tbsp freshly squeezed lime juice

handful of cracked ice

fine lime rind strips (see Cook's Tip, page 82), to decorate

Melon margaritas

1 small flavorful cantaloupe melon, peeled, seeded, and diced

several large handfuls of ice

juice of 1 lime

scant ½ cup tequila

sugar, to taste

Frozen peach margaritas

1 peach, pitted, peeled, sliced, and frozen, or an equal amount of ready-frozen peaches

¼ cup tequila

¼ cup peach or orange-flavored liqueur

juice of ½ lime

1–2 tbsp fresh peach or orange juice, if needed

Method

❶ To make the Classic Margaritas, moisten the rim of 2 shallow, stemmed glasses with the lime rind, then dip the edge of the glasses in salt. Shake off the excess.

❷ Place the tequila in a food processor or blender with the liqueur, lime juice, and cracked ice. Process to blend well.

❸ If preferred, strain the drink before pouring into the prepared glasses, taking care not to disturb the salt-coated rim. Decorate with lime rind strips and serve.

❹ To make the Melon Margaritas, place the melon in a food processor or blender and process to a purée. Add the ice, lime juice, tequila, and sugar to taste and process until smooth. Pour into chilled shallow glasses and serve.

❺ To make the Frozen Peach Margaritas, blend the frozen fruit, tequila, liqueur, and lime juice in a food processor or blender to a thick purée. If too thick, add a little peach juice. Pour into chilled, shallow glasses and serve.

Fruity Refreshers

These fragrant, utterly refreshing drinks are full of the tropical flavors of Mexico.
They cool and revive with each sip.

serves 4–6

Coconut-lime drink

1¾ cups coconut milk (unsweetened)

½ cup freshly squeezed lime juice

4 cups tropical fruit juice, such as mango,

papaya, guava, or passion fruit

sugar, to taste

crushed ice

fresh mint sprigs, to decorate

Sangria

1 bottle full-bodied dry red wine

¼ cup orange-flavored liqueur

¼ cup brandy

1 cup orange juice

sugar, to taste

1 orange, washed

1 lime, washed

1 peach or nectarine

½ cucumber, thinly sliced

ice cubes

sparkling mineral water, for topping up

Method

❶ To make the Coconut-Lime Drink, combine the coconut milk with the lime juice, tropical fruit juice, and sugar to taste in a large, nonmetallic bowl. Add the ice and whisk until well mixed. Alternatively, place the ingredients in a food processor or blender and process until well mixed. Pour into tall glasses and serve at once, decorated with mint sprigs.

❷ To make the Sangria, pour the wine into a punch bowl and mix in the liqueur, brandy, orange juice, and sugar to taste. Cover and chill for at least 2 hours.

❸ Just before serving, slice the orange and lime widthwise. Cut the peach in half and remove the pit, then slice the flesh.

❹ Remove the punch bowl from the refrigerator. Add the prepared fruit, cucumber, and ice cubes and top up with sparkling mineral water. Serve at once.

Cook's tip

To turn the Coconut-Lime Drink into an alcoholic cocktail, add 2 tablespoons of white rum per person. Add an extra decoration of tropical fruit pieces, threaded onto bamboo skewers.

Recipe List

- Authentic Guacamole *26* • Aztec Oranges *82* • Beef & Vegetable Soup *12*

- Black Bean Nachos *18* • Buñuelo Stars *90* • Burritos of Lamb & Black Beans *58*

- Carnitas *52* • Cheese & Bean Quesadillas *16* • Cheese Enchiladas with Mole Flavors *74*

- Chicken Breasts in Green Salsa with Sour Cream *38*

- Chicken Tostadas with Green Salsa & Chipotle *46*

- Chile-Marinated Shrimp with Avocado Sauce *66* • Chile Verde *56*

- Chorizo & Artichoke Heart Quesadillas *22* • Churros *88*

- Citrus-Marinated Chicken *40* • Classic Beef Fajitas *48* • Classic Margaritas *92*

- Fish with Yucatan Flavors *64* • Fresh Pineapple Salsa *30* • Fruity Refreshers *94*

- Green Chile & Chicken Chilaquiles *44* • Hot Tomato Sauce *32* • Icy Fruit Blizzard *78*

- Mexican Chocolate Meringues *86* • Mexican Vegetable Soup with Tortilla Chips *14*

- Michoacan Beef *50* • Migas *68* • Mole Poblano *28* • Pineapple with Tequila & Mint *80*

- Refried Beans *34* • Rice with Black Beans *70* • Sincronizadas *20*

- Spicy Broiled Salmon *62* • Spicy Gazpacho *10* • Spicy Meat & Chipotle Hash *60*

- Spicy Pork with Prunes *54* • Strawberries & Oranges with Lime *84*

- Tequila-Marinated Crispy Chicken Wings *42* • Two Classic Salsas *24*

- Vegetable Tostadas *72*